Rising Parent Media, LLC
© 2017 by Rising Parent Media
All rights reserved. Published 2017
Printed in the United States of America

20 19 18 17 16   1 2 3 4

ISBN: 978-0-9987312-5-4

The paper used in this publication meets the minimum requirements of the American National Standard for Information Sciences—Permanence of Paper for Printed Library Materials, ANSI Z39.48-1992.

FOR GREAT RESOURCES AND INFORMATION, FOLLOW US ON OUR SOCIAL MEDIA OUTLETS:

Facebook: www.facebook.com/educateempowerkids/
Twitter: @EduEmpowerKids
Pinterest: pinterest.com/educateempower/
Instagram: Eduempowerkids

www.educateempowerkids.org

NOAH'S NEW PHONE
A STORY ABOUT USING TECHNOLOGY FOR GOOD

Educate and Empower Kids would like to acknowledge the following people who contributed time, talents, and energy to this publication.

STORY BY:
Dina Alexander, MS

EDITED BY:
Maren Warner
Jenny Webb, MA
Tina Mattsson

DESIGN AND ILLUSTRATION BY:
Jera Mehrdad

SPECIAL THANKS TO:
Kyle Roberts, MA
Melody Bergman
Cliff Park, MBA
Byran Korth, Ph.D.

POSITIVE DIGITAL CITIZENSHIP: Using technology to make a positive impact on others.

SOCIAL MEDIA: Websites and apps that people use to share information and develop personal and professional relationships. Facebook, Google+, Instagram, Pinterest, Snapchat, and Twitter are examples of social media.

INTRODUCTION

We have created a world full of technology, and every human is affected by its power and influence—especially kids! Each time we text, send an email, post on social media, interact with others on a game, or create a new piece of technology, we create ripples.

All of our actions online and in "real life" create ripples, or small waves of change around us. Make sure you are the same person in both places, whether you think someone is watching or not.

To get the most out of this book, **READ** it with your child, **DISCUSS** several of the questions provided at the end of the story, and, if possible, do an **ACTIVITY** together. Engaging with your child this way will create a richer learning experience!

Noah couldn't believe his good fortune. His parents had finally given him his very own smart phone.

"This is so awesome! I can finally text and play games like my friends," he thought happily.

Every day, he woke up excited to hear his phone's alarm. He liked to scroll through his phone first thing, even before he rolled out of bed—until his mom would say it was almost time to leave for the bus.

His friends wasted no time showing him new games to download and videos to watch.

His big sister taught him how to follow "friends" and famous people on social media.

Standing at the bus stop one morning, Noah looked up from his phone.

"How long have I been staring at my phone?" he wondered.

Everyone stood in silence, staring at their phones.

No one talked to each other.

A sense of uneasiness prickled at his chest. When was the last time they talked to each other at the bus stop?

What was happening to everyone? They looked different.

"Do I look different? Am I different now that I have a phone?" he thought, puzzled.

Noah thought about the past few weeks.

He was surprised to realize that his phone had already changed his life.

It had changed his free time.

It had changed his relationships.

It had changed who his "friends" were.

It had changed how he expressed himself.

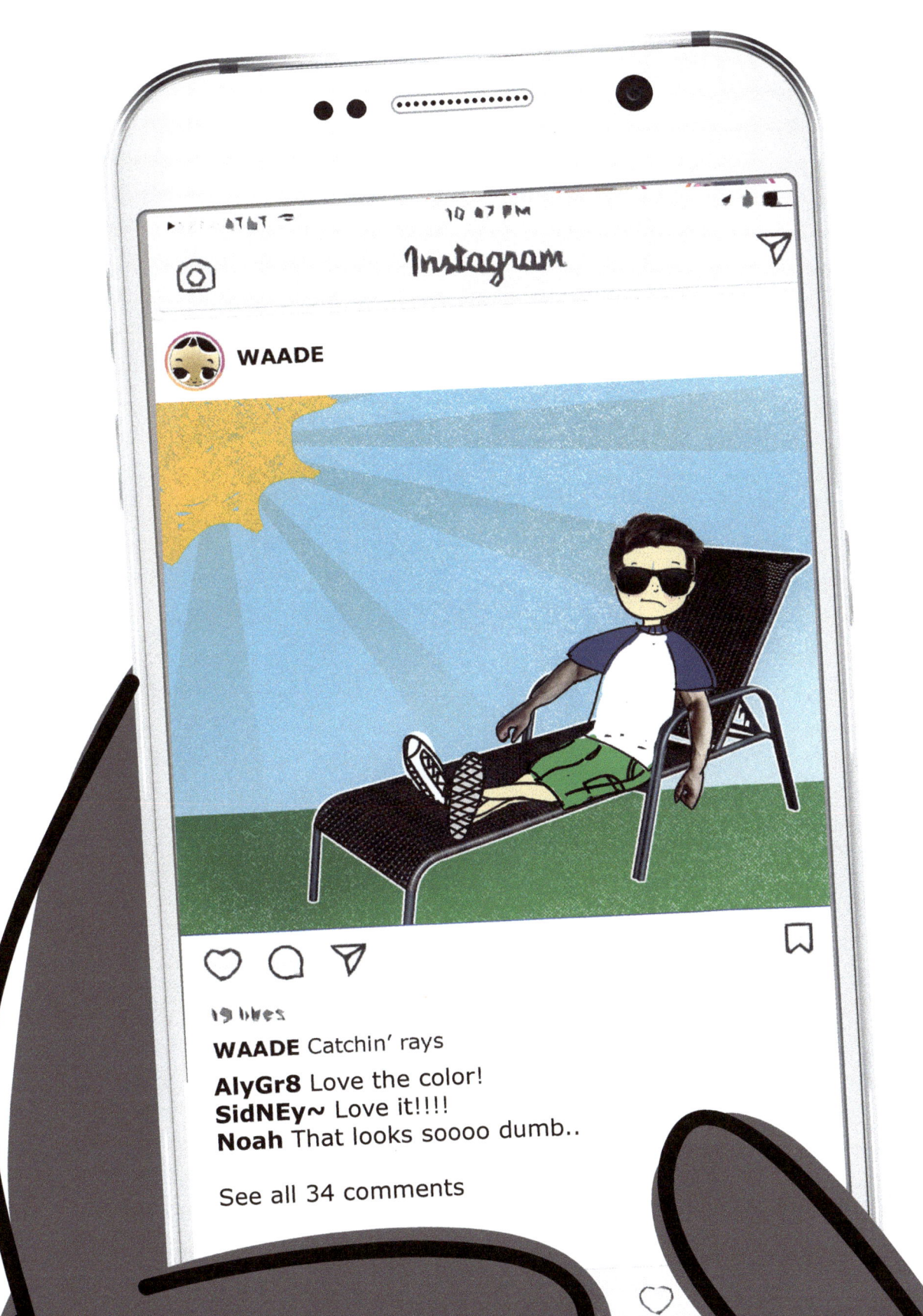

He used to laugh out loud with his friends, not just LOL by himself.

In fact,
he couldn't think
of a time
in the past month
where he hadn't
reached for his phone

when he was bored,

when he was lonely,

or when he felt an unpleasant feeling coming on.

It reminded him of his favorite blanket when he was a little boy.

Was his phone just a big-kid pacifier?

Something to distract or comfort him?

A toy to entertain him?

He thought about his parents and teachers.

Were their phones just adult pacifiers?

As the bus pulled up, the prickle in his chest became stronger. He remembered how just last week he had posted a photo of a classmate eating his lunch with a caption that said, "Oink, oink."

The kid seemed upset and glared at Noah all day. "What a baby," Noah thought, rolling his eyes.

Noah pushed these thoughts away and boarded the bus.

Staring down at his phone, Noah began drinking from his water bottle. He was so distracted, he didn't notice when the bottle started leaking onto his pants.

When he got up to exit the bus, an older kid laughed and pointed out that his pants were wet. Noah quickly covered the front of his pants with his backpack.

When he got to class, he hastily put his backpack down and scooted close to his desk, hoping that no one else would notice his wet pants.

Within the hour, his pants were dry and the incident was forgotten.

Lunchtime arrived, and he walked into the cafeteria. He felt an odd knot in his chest and stomach as he looked around. Noah realized most of the other kids were staring at him.

Turning around, he saw several kids at different tables laughing and pointing at him. Confused and uneasy, he paid for his lunch and sat down at his usual table.

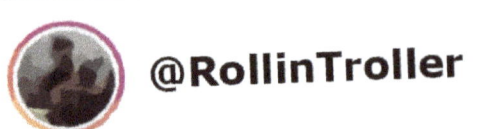

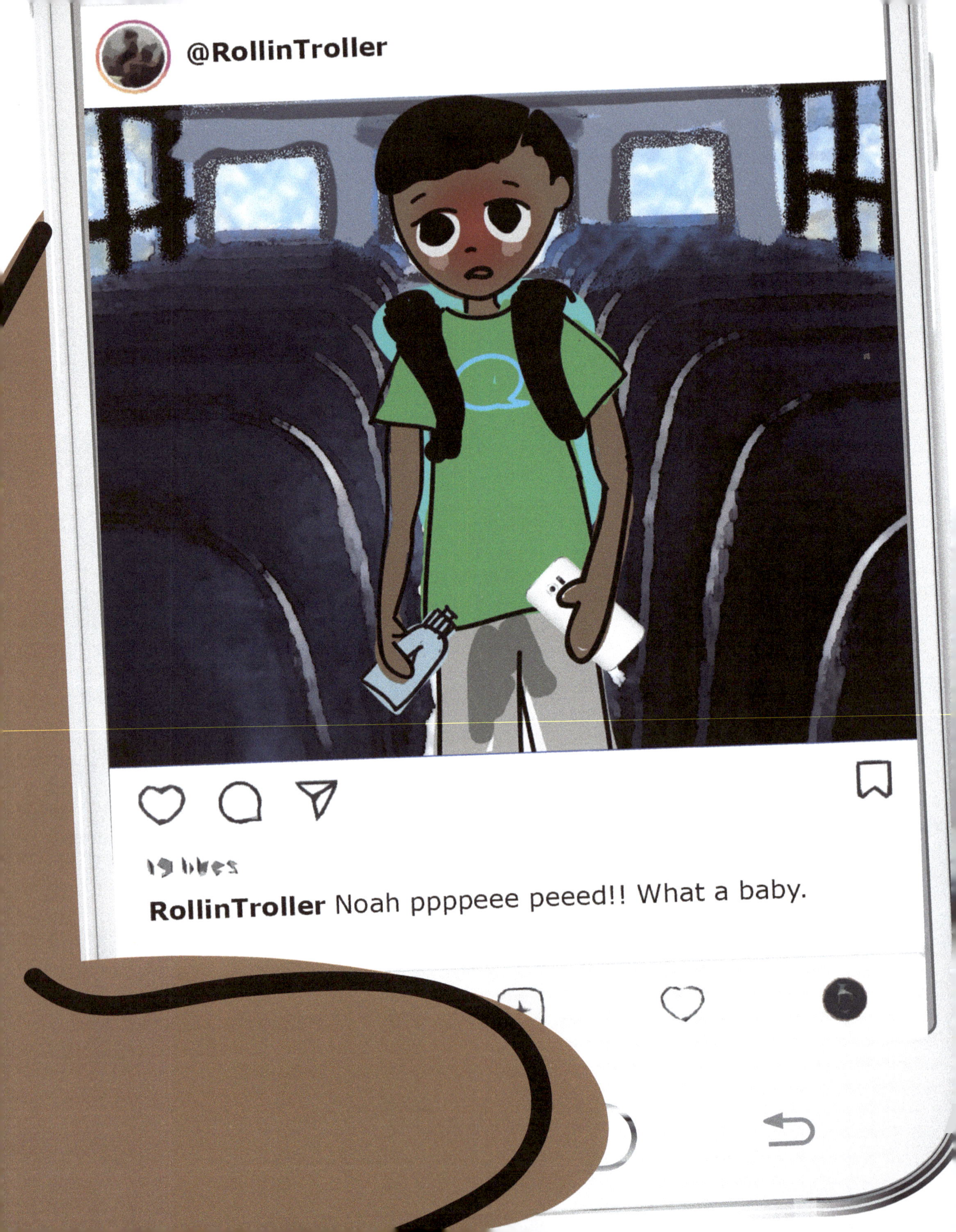
@RollinTroller
19 likes
RollinTroller Noah ppppeee peeed!! What a baby.

His friend Kennedy leaned over toward him. "Did you see this?"

Noah looked down at Kennedy's phone. To his horror, for the whole world to see on social media, there was a picture of Noah with his pants wet, standing in the aisle of the bus.

Under the photo was a caption that said, "What a baby!"

Noah's heart sank. He felt sick. He felt like crying. He wanted to run out of the cafeteria and keep running until he got home.

"It was just my leaky water bottle," he stammered out to Kennedy.

"I know," said Kennedy sympathetically. "Mine leaks sometimes too."

"I'm so sorry someone did that to you."

Noah looked around the room. Other kids were looking at him, some with laughter in their eyes, others with empathy.

"I can't tell who did it," Kennedy said. "I don't recognize that account."

Clicking on the account, Noah could tell that the account was fake. He knew people sometimes created accounts like these to hide their identity when they posted something mean.

"What are you going to do about it?" asked Kennedy.

"I don't know," replied Noah. Thoughts swirled through his mind.

Should he tell a teacher?
Should he talk to his parents?

The rest of the school day was a blur. When he got home he avoided his mom and her usual questions about school that day. Alone in his room, his stomach twisted as he thought about the whole day.

Inside his room, Noah felt alone and isolated. He hadn't hung out with his friends since getting his phone. He didn't feel he could just call or visit them. Everyone seemed so busy with homework, sports practice, or texting and scrolling on their phones.

And this wasn't something he wanted to text about.

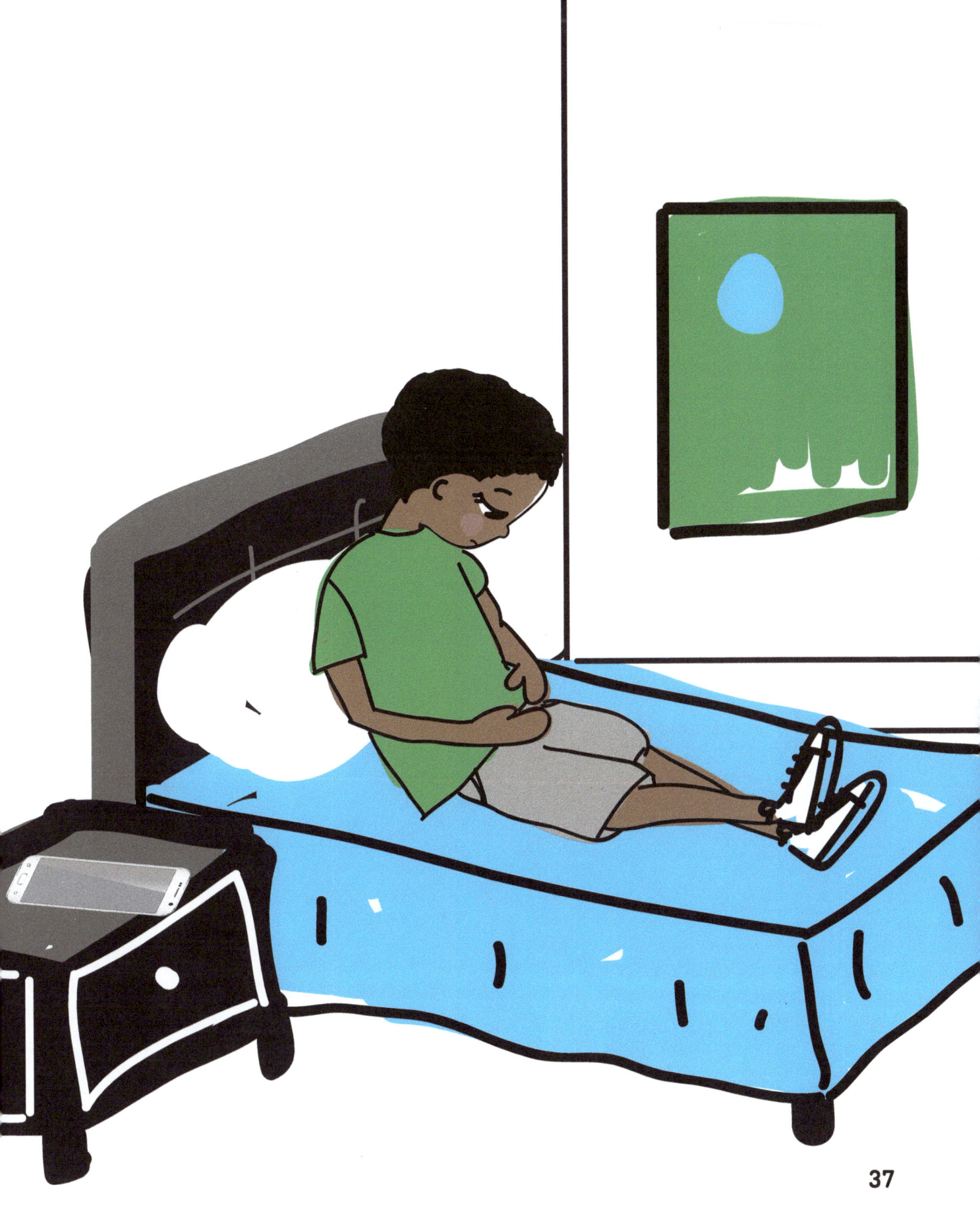

Noah thought about how he and his friends just stared at their phones every day before and after school. He realized that he stared at his phone between bits of homework, after homework, after dinner, and even in bed.

Now he was the target of someone's "joke."

By the time dinner started, however, Noah was angry. He felt betrayed, as if a cherished pet had suddenly bit him. Was this all phones and tablets were good for?

Did he want to get rid of his phone? No. But there had to be something more to this technology.

Something BETTER.

Noah's mom noticed how quiet he was being. She asked, "What's the matter?" and the whole story came tumbling out.

All the kids staring creepily at their phones, the water bottle, the photo, and the horrible lunchtime.

The more he talked, the angrier Dad looked and the more sympathetic mom became. Noah's parents were kind enough to not mention, right at this moment, the trouble he had gotten into last week when he posted another kid's picture.

Mom got up and put her arms around Noah.

"What do you want to do about this?" Dad asked.

"I haven't decided yet," Noah replied truthfully. "I just don't understand. Is this all phones and computers were made for? Playing games, watching videos, and making fun of each other on social media?"

"Do you really think that's all these devices can do?" Mom asked gently.

"I don't know. I guess I can do homework with my computer too," he said, shrugging.

"Think about it Noah," Mom encouraged. "Is there more you can do with all of this technology?"

In the morning, Noah approached the bus stop with some apprehension, expecting more pointing and laughter. Once again everyone was more interested in their phones.

He could hear his mom's question in his head.

"Is there more you can do with all of this technology?"

Since no one seemed interested in talking, Noah pulled out his phone and started scrolling through his social media feed. He saw Kennedy's latest post. It was a selfie Kennedy had taken of the two of them.

The knot in Noah's stomach loosened up a bit.

He decided to post his own photo. He found one he had taken last week after school with Kennedy and some other friends. Instead of his usual one line caption, Noah wrote a sincere compliment about each person in the photo and tagged them.

Noah walked into school as a stream of encouraging texts lit up his phone. He was too busy replying to notice the few snickers and fingers pointing in his direction.

The uneasiness in Noah's chest lightened.

It hadn't been a big deal to use his phone to compliment his friends, and Noah was amazed how quickly that small choice caused positive ripples in his own life.

In science class, Noah saw online images of supernovas and planets thousands of light years away.

In social studies, his class connected with another class on the other side of the country in an online video chat.

During lunch, excitement filled Noah as he and his friends watched a video of how to create an awesome village in Minecraft.

After school, when a friend needed help with homework, Noah showed him a useful new app.

When Noah got home from school his mom asked her usual questions about how school was that day.

"Better," said Noah.

"Did you think about what I said last night?" she asked.

As he thought about his day, a grin spread across his face.

"Yeah, I really did," he said. "Hey mom, technology isn't really good or bad, is it?"

"Not really, no," his mom replied, smiling.

Noah nodded.

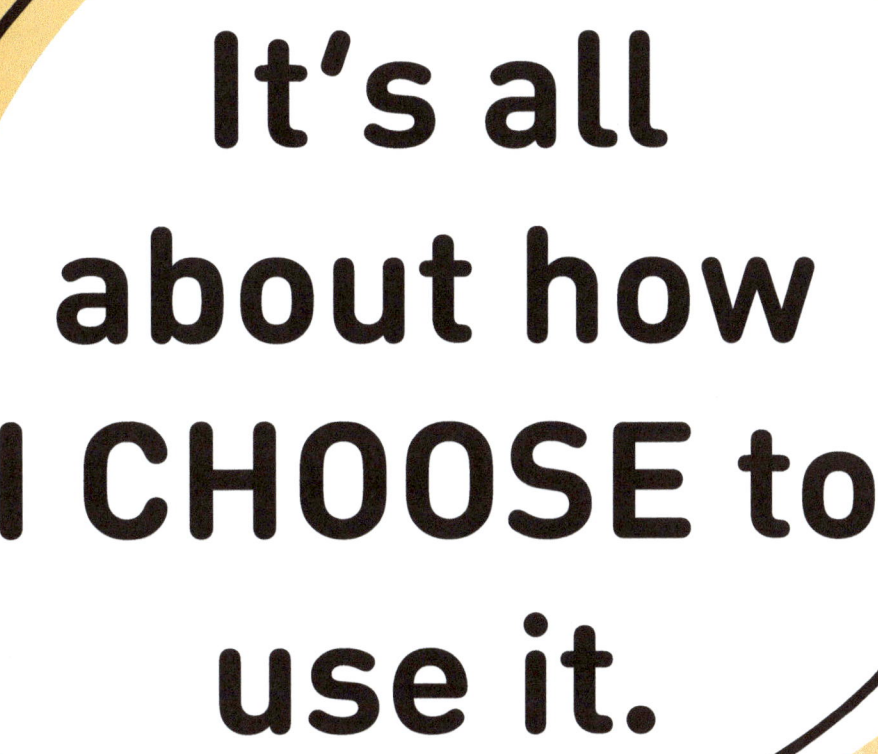

What kind of ripples will you

CHOOSE to make today?

WORKBOOK

This is a great opportunity to talk about the enormous power kids and adults hold within their smartphones. Use the following questions and activities to discuss the story, the great potential there is in technology, and some healthy tech boundaries we can practice. Remember, these questions do not necessarily have right or wrong answers.

> Be a great DIGITAL CITIZEN by using technology to enhance your family, school, and community through tolerance, kindness, authenticity, and ingenuity.

DISCUSSION QUESTIONS

FROM THE STORY:
Noah received a smartphone for his 11th birthday.

- Is this is the right age for someone to receive a phone from his parents?
- If not, when is the right time for someone to own a smartphone?
- What was the uneasiness that pricked in Noah's chest as he looked at the other kids at the bus stop?

Let's pretend that the kid who posted the photo of Noah was also the same kid that Noah posted an unflattering photo of eating his lunch.

- Would he be justified in posting an unkind photo of Noah?
- If someone posted an embarrassing photo of you on social media, what would you do?
- Do you have a friend like Kennedy who would help and support you in a tough situation at school?

Noah could have been vengeful and tried to find and hurt the person who posted the mean photo of him.

- Why did you think Noah decided to do something kind instead?
- How did Noah feel when he sincerely complimented his friends online?

THE POTENTIAL FOR TECHNOLOGY:

There are many benefits to people owning a smartphone. It is easier to connect and communicate with family and friends, build business relationships, map a trip, and get information instantly.

Noah found it easy to use his phone to make fun of others.
What are some ways we can damage others through technology?

Noah soon realized he could do so much more with his smartphone than scroll through social media and make fun of other people online.

- What are some things he could do?
- What are some things you can do with a smartphone, tablet, or computer?
- What can you learn, teach others, and create?

Technology has made it easier to reach out to presidents, senators, mayors, favorite authors, experts, celebrities, and other influential people through email or social media.

- Who would you like to connect with and why?

Websites, forums, and social media make it possible to connect with organizations and people who care about the same things you might care about (animals, sports, the environment, assisting refugees, etc.)

- What groups and individuals would you like to join or learn more about?

Our actions online and in "real life" create ripples, or small waves of change around us. Make sure you are creating positive ripples by complimenting others on social media, being respectful even when you disagree with someone, standing up for others, reporting bullying, and listening to others' opinions.

- What are more ways we can help and uplift others and create positive ripples with technology?
- Are you the same person online that you are in "real life"?
- Technology is powerful! How can you change the world using technology?

HEALTHY BOUNDARIES:

Phones and other devices have many uses such as texting, talking, gaming, posting on social media, doing homework, researching, reading the news, emailing, etc. However, some people spend far too much time on their phones or in front of screens.

- What is a healthy amount of time to spend in front of a screen each day?
- If you have a phone, what are some things you use it for?
- What are some ways your siblings and parents use their phones?
- How much texting or posting on social media in one day is too much?
- Do you have "device free" time? For example, do you put phones and tablets away at dinner time?

Noah realized he was on his phone every time he got bored, lonely, sad, or when feeling unpleasant.

- Do you use your phone in this way?

- Is this okay?
- What are other things you can do when you feel this way?

Kids and adults spend a lot of time playing video games on smartphones, tablets, and computers.

- Can lessons be learned while gaming?
- Is there value in construction-based games like Minecraft?
- Can gaming together with siblings or family members build family relationships?
- Is gaming a positive coping skill (a way to relax or process stress)?

Everyone seems to own a smartphone.

What are potential benefits of so many people owning smartphones? (Ease in communication, use of GPS to map a trip, get information quickly, etc.)

What are potential setbacks of so many people owning smartphones? (Fewer in-person conversations, loss of empathy, inability to wait, loss of patience, etc.)

STAYING SAFE:
With technology being easily accessible to kids through smartphones, tablets, and computers, they are also easily exposed to violence, sexual imagery, and online predators.

Is your family having open conversations about online safety and some of the dangers encountered on the internet?

Predators will always "go" where kids are. And kids are online now.

How can we protect ourselves, our kids, and our personal information from predators? How else do we stay safe online?

- It is important, as families, to discuss and set guidelines for age appropriate online use and the amount of time spent on devices.
- What is an appropriate age for kids to receive a smartphone or use social media?
- What is appropriate use and behavior while using devices in your home, at school, and at work?
- What is appropriate use and behavior on social media?
- What behavior is not okay?
- What are the dangers of becoming "addicted" to technology?
- What negative behavior should we report to parents or teachers?
- When is "mean" behavior really bullying?

ACTIVITY:

Challenge your family to make their media interactions more positive. Set a goal to post only positive things for one week. Encourage family members to share uplifting, informative, or humorous examples.

Find a game on one of your devices that encourages you to interact or work together with other people, in person.

Create a Facebook or Instagram account for your friends or school that you use to compliment each other or encourage each other.

CHALLENGE:

Choose a project or movement that you can join. Use technology to assist you in organizing and/or carrying out your work.

EXAMPLES: Use Facebook or Instagram to invite others and organize a fundraiser for a local charity.

Create a petition on change.org to eliminate plastic bags in your local community.

Share a video or post that draws awareness to the plight of people struggling (refugees, the homeless, hungry children, etc.).

Learn how to stop online bullying on iwitnessbullying.org. Make a commitment to be a good digital citizen, and stand up for the victim if you see someone being mistreated online.

TIPS FOR PARENTS AND TEACHERS:

Help your kids see potential in all technology. Start looking for ways to use phones, tablets, etc. as tools and instruments, not just as a way to pacify or entertain us. Help your children see themselves as agents for change. Remind them that they can change the world for the better!

Look for opportunities to use technology to help others.

Openly discuss rules and guidelines for cellphone usage for kids and parents in your home. Make rules together.

Create a cellphone contract for your child or download one from the the internet. Look it over, discuss it with your child, and have your child commit to following the rules laid out in the contract.

Take the next step in changing the world around you. Look for opportunities to co-create new technology, new positive, online trends, new platforms, new devices, and anything else you can imagine together with your kids.

GLOSSARY:

App: An application. Typically a small, specialized program downloaded onto mobile devices.

Digital Citizenship: Appropriate and responsible behavior with regards to technology use.

Positive Digital Citizenship: Using technology to make a positive impact on others (family, school, community, etc.) through tolerance, kindness, authenticity, and ingenuity.

Ripples: A small wave that moves outward. We create ripples when we create small changes that affect those around us. These small changes can continue through our families, communities, and the whole world.

Social Media: Websites and apps that people use to share information and develop personal and professional relationships. Facebook, Google+, Instagram, Pinterest, Snapchat, and Twitter are examples of social media.

RESOURCES:

These websites can help you discuss and practice positive digital citizenship in your home or school:

For Adults and Kids:
Educate and Empower Kids: educateempowerkids.org
Digital Citizenship Institute: http://www.digitalcitizenshipinstitute.com
Digital Citizenship Utah: http://digcitutah.com
EPIK Deliberate Digital: http://www.epik.org
InCtrl: http://www.teachinctrl.org

For Kids:
DigCitKids: http://www.digcitkids.com

CITATIONS:

A Lesson About Using Technology for Good. (2016, December 31). Retrieved July 1, 2017, from https://educateempowerkids.org/lesson-using-technology-good.

App. (n.d.). Retrieved July 19, 2017, from http://www.dictionary.com/browse/app.

Digital Citizenship. (n.d.). Retrieved July 27, 2017, from http://www.digitalcitizenship.net/.

Shipp, J. (n.d.). The Teen Cell Phone Contract. Retrieved August 25, 2017, from http://joshshipp.com/wp-content/uploads/2016/09/teenage-cell-phone-agreement.pdf.
josh shipp.com

Talking to Your Kids About Addiction. (2017, May 31). Retrieved July 20, 2017, from https://educateempowerkids.org/talking-kids-addiction.

EDUCATEEMPOWERKIDS.ORG

If you enjoyed this book, please leave a positive review on amazon.com

For great resources and information, follow us on our social media outlets:

Facebook: www.facebook.com/educateempowerkids/
Twitter: @EduEmpowerKids
Pinterest: pinterest.com/educateempower/
Instagram: Eduempowerkids

Subscribe to our website for exclusive offers and information at:
www.educateempowerkids.org

www.ingramcontent.com/pod-product-compliance
Lightning Source LLC
Chambersburg PA
CBHW040046100526
44584CB00034BA/4480